Talking Hands
AT WORK

EN EL TRABAJO

WRITTEN BY KATHLEEN PETELINSEK AND E. RUSSELL PRIMM
ILLUSTRATED BY JULIA GOOZEN

A SPECIAL THANKS TO OUR ADVISERS: JUNE PRUSAK IS A DEAF THERAPEUTIC RECREATOR WHO
BELIEVES IN THE MOTTO "LIFE IS GOOD," REGARDLESS OF YOUR ABILITY TO HEAR.

CARMINE L. VOZZOLO IS AN EDUCATOR OF CHILDREN WHO ARE DEAF
AND HARD OF HEARING, AS WELL AS THEIR FAMILIES.

The Child's World

Published in the United States of America by The Child's World®
PO Box 326, Chanhassen, MN 55317-0326
800-599-READ
www.childsworld.com

Cover/frontispiece: Image Source.

Interior: 3, 4, 6, 8, 11, 13, 17, 18, 20, 21, 23—RubberBall Productions;
5, 9, 16—Comstock Images; 7, 12, 14, 15—Image Source; 10—Stockdisc;
19—Corbis; 22—RubberBall Productions/Getty Images.

The Child's World®: Mary Berendes, Publishing Director

Editorial Directions, Inc.: E. Russell Primm, Editorial Director; Katie Marsico,
Managing Editor; Judith Shiffer, Associate Editor; Caroline Wood, Editorial
Assistant; Javier Millán, Proofreader; Cian Laughlin O'Day, Photo Researcher
and Selector

The Design Lab: Kathleen Petelinsek, Art Director; Julia Goozen, Art
Production

LIBRARY OF CONGRESS CATALOGING-IN-PUBLICATION DATA
Petelinsek, Kathleen.
  At work / = En el trabajo / by Kathleen Petelinsek and E. Russell Primm.
      p. cm. – (Talking hands)
  In English and Spanish.
  ISBN 1-59296-451-6 (lib. bdg. : alk. paper)
1. American Sign Language—Juvenile literature. 2. Work—Juvenile literature.
I. Title: En el trabajo. II. Primm, E. Russell, 1958– III. Title.
  HV2476.P4725 2006
  419'.7–dc22   2005027105

NOTE TO PARENTS AND EDUCATORS:

The understanding of any language begins with the acquisition of vocabulary, whether the language is spoken or manual. The books in the Talking Hands series provide readers, both young and old, with a first introduction to basic American Sign Language signs. Combining close photo cues and simple, but detailed, line illustration, children and adults alike can begin the process of learning American Sign Language. In addition to the English word and sign for that word, we have included the Spanish word. The addition of the Spanish word is a wonderful way to allow children to see multiple ways (English, Spanish, signed) to say the same word. This is also beneficial for Spanish-speaking families to learn the sign even though they may not know the English word for that object.

Let these books be an introduction to the world of American Sign Language. Most languages have regional dialects and multiple ways of expressing the same thought. This is also true for sign language. We have attempted to use the most common version of the signs for the words in this series. As with any language, the best way to learn is to be taught in person by a frequent user. It is our hope that this series will pique your interest in sign language.

Pilot
Piloto

1.

2.

Teacher
Maestra

1.

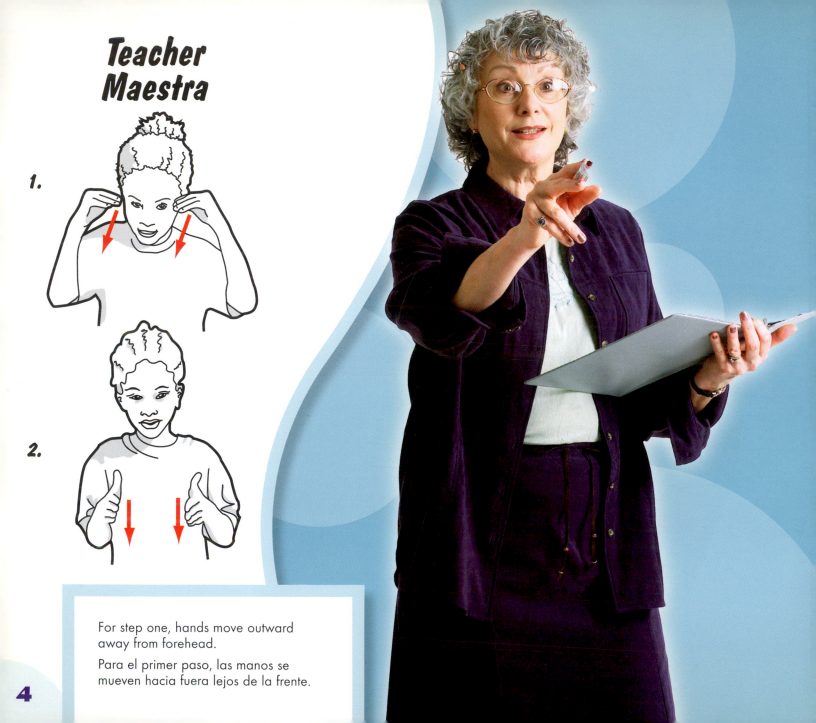

2.

For step one, hands move outward away from forehead.

Para el primer paso, las manos se mueven hacia fuera lejos de la frente.

Carpenter
Carpintero

1.

2.

Nurse
Enfermero

1.

Right hand makes the letter "N" and taps left wrist twice.

La mano derecha hace la letra "N" y golpea ligeramente la muñeca izquierda dos veces.

Principal
Principal

1.

Right hand makes the letter "P" and circles around and then touches the back of left hand.

La mano derecha hace la letra "P" y circula alrededor y después toca la parte posterior de la mano izquierda.

Painter
Pintor

1.

2.

3.

For steps one and two, right hand moves up and down, similar to a paintbrush, against left hand.

Para el primer y segundo paso, la mano derecha se mueve hacia arriba y hacia abajo, similar a una brocha, contra la mano izquierda.

Soldier
Soldado

1.

Hands make the letter "A." Right hand taps chest twice, and left hand taps ribs twice. Both hands tap body at the same time.

Las manos hacen la letra "A." La mano derecha golpea ligeramente el pecho dos veces, y la mano izquierda golpea ligeramente las costillas dos veces. Las dos manos golpean ligeramente el cuerpo a la misma vez.

Librarian
Bibliotecaria

1.

2.

For step one, right hand makes the letter "L" and circles clockwise.

Para el primer paso, la mano derecha hace la letra "L" y circula a la derecha.

Police Officer
Policía

1.

Right hand makes the letter "C" and taps upper left chest to represent a police badge.

La mano derecha hace la letra "C" y golpea ligeramente el lado izquierdo del pecho superior representando la placa de un policía.

Cashier
Cajera

1.

2.

For step one, wiggle fingers as if using a cash register.

Para el primer paso, menee los dedos como si estuviera usando una caja registradora.

Cook
Cocinero

1.

2.

3.

For steps one and two, flip right hand, palm down, to palm up on left hand.

Para el primer y segundo paso, voltee la mano derecha, palma hacia abajo, a la palma para arriba en la mano izquierda.

Lawyer
Abogado

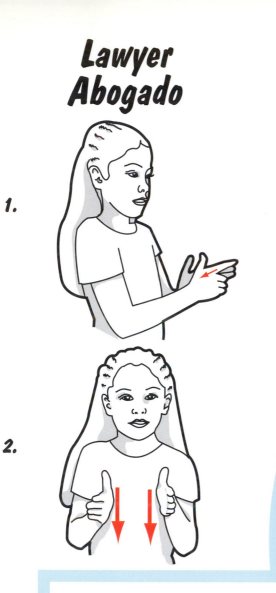

1.

2.

For step one, right hand makes the letter "L" and moves along flat left hand from fingers to palm.

Para el primer paso, la mano derecha hace la letra "L" y se mueve a lo largo de la mano izquierda desde los dedos hasta la palma.

Judge
Juez

1.

Mimic banging a gavel.
Imite golpear con martillo.

17

Artist
Artista

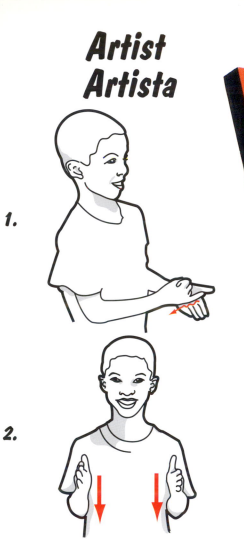

1.

2.

For step one, right hand makes the letter "I" and moves in a squiggly line down left hand.

Para el primer paso, la mano derecha hace la letra "I" y se mueve como una línea retorcida hacia abajo en la mano izquierda.

Actor
Agente

1.

2.

For step one, hands make the letter "A" and alternately rotate in front of chest. Thumbs brush downward on chest during rotation.

Para el primer paso, las manos hacen la letra "A" y alternativamente rotan delante de pecho. Los pulgares rozan hacia abajo el pecho durante la rotación.

Coach
Entrenador

1.

Right hand makes the letter "C" and taps right shoulder twice.

La mano derecha hace la letra "C" y golpea ligeramente el hombro derecho dos veces.

Firefighter
Bombero

1.

Right hand makes the letter "B" and taps forehead.

La mano derecha hace la letra "B" y golpea ligeramente la frente.

Dancer
Bailarín

1.

2.

For step one, right hand makes the letter "V" and swings back and forth over left hand.

Para el primer paso, la mano derecha hace la letra "V" y se mece adelante y hacia atrás sobre la mano izquierda.

Farmer
Granjero

1.

2.

3.

For step one and two, open right hand moves from left side of chin to right side.

Para el primer y segundo paso, la mano derecha abierta se mueve del lado izquierdo de la barilla hacia el lado derecho.

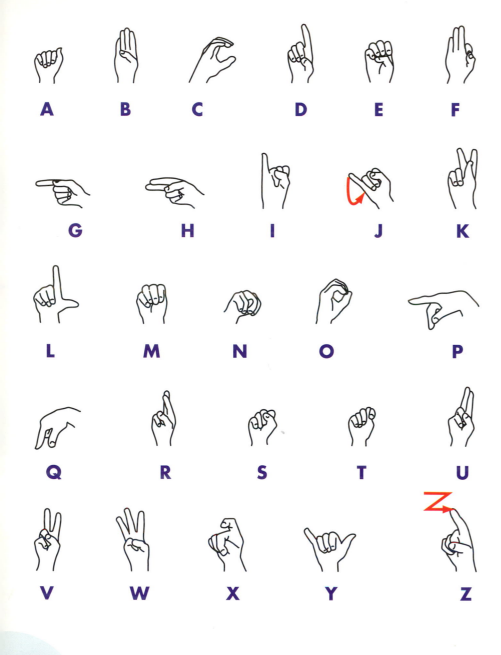

A B C D E F

G H I J K

L M N O P

Q R S T U

V W X Y Z

A SPECIAL THANK-YOU
to our models from the Alexander Graham Bell Elementary School in Chicago, Illinois:

Alina is seven years old and is in the second grade. Her favorite things to do are art, soccer, and swimming. DJ is her brother!

Dareous has seven brothers and sisters. He likes football. His favorite team is the Detroit Lions. He also likes to play with his Gameboy and Playstation.

Darionna is seven and is in the second grade. She has two sisters. She likes the swings and merry-go-round on the playground. She also loves art.

DJ is eight years old and is in the third grade. He loves playing the harmonica and his Gameboy. Alina is his sister!

Jasmine is seven years old and is in the second grade. She likes writing and math in school. She also loves to swim.